BECOME THE NEXT ONLINE STAR!

For kick-ass women who want fame, fortune and success.

By Camilla Kristiansen

http://camillakristiansen.com

Get your free gift here:

https://camillakristiansen.com/freegift/

For the women out there who feel that they don't have a chance. You do. Go for it now! Dedicated to my girls Amanda & Vanessa, dream big and know that you both can have it all!

TABLE OF CONTENTS

CHAPTER 1: MAKE MONEY!

For years I hated myself. I wanted to have my own business and live a life on my own terms. That was not going to happen for sure. I was locked in a safe corporate jobs 3 times. I tried once, after 3 years as an accountant to break free, but I was scared. I was scare of how I could make money from doing things I love. And back then I did not know what I loved doing. I was just coping like all the others and playing it safe going to a job day after day that I did not like that much.

But to live a life, that it safe and secure, you have to have some form of money coming your way. That's for sure. Or else how are you going to pay your bills, pay for food, take care of your family? It took me 13 years before I was really ready to kiss my fears goodbye and go after my dreams full-time. I knew that this path as an entrepreneur was not an easy one. But the first thing you have to do is to love yourself. What has that to do with making money you think?

Everything. Everything in life has to do with you not loving yourself enough. You are good enough and you have to learn to love YOU, then when you really love yourself, money will flow. You will ooze of self-love but not in a vanity way. You will show others how they also can love themselves and be happy. Life is easy when you don't feed your brain with negative thoughts on how you have to act to be liked by everyone else.

You are here on earth for 2 reasons. Nr 1 you have to love yourself and then everything in your life will change, also your money situation. Nr 2 you have to live life fearless. When you love yourself and others, you will never put yourself in a situation that is not safe for you or your loved ones. Then you can go into life without fear and be an online star. The one that we have been waiting for. You have a gift that no one else has. Yes, they talk about strategies and how to do this and that and how to make 10K in 10 days.

Making money is easy when you love yourself, love what you do and be fearless. You don't fear how your next project is gonna work out. If this really comes from your heart and is a «Hell Yes» project then you will have success, and with success comes money. This book is written for you who really are tired of all the crap out there on how you must follow some kind of strategies to make it online.

You can build your business up again from scratch and make money from day 1. There are no strategies that will work. They try to tell you. I have tried them all. I am sick and tired of following strategies that doesn't work. What is working is you. You work when you love yourself, know yourself and put your fears aside and put your best work to place. Ask yourself what you really want to make money from doing in your business? What is it that you would love to do all day long? For me it's writing books, blogs, making videos and coaching women into finding their true passion.

Then I just do it. I don't ask for permission to be an author. I am. I don't ask others how I should talk in my videos. I just do it. So should you. Go after the things you love in life and that is the thing that will make you money, give you fame, fortune and success. If you want to be the next online star out there, then you can definitive do it. Who else is talking about fuck the rules and just be yourself? No one. They all sell strategies after strategies that don't work and believe me in the end it can't work forever. People will start to question it if the only thing they sell is strategies.

I want you to sell YOU. But how can I make money from being myself you ask? Well, there are no one else like you and you have a message that people need. What it is that comes so easy for you that you can't help it? What do you believe in so bad that you have to get it out of your mind and tell others about it? That is what's gonna make you money, the thing you love talking about, doing, breathing.

How you sell it doesn't matter. The thing that matters is that you show up and take a step towards your dreams in life.

You have to love yourself enough so that you can give your all in your business, life and with your loved ones. No one is put here on earth to suffer. If you now feel that you are a failure, then think again. You are put here on earth to be something to others. You have a gift that you will make money from. How you find your tribe? Call them in. Market to them. Those you love working with.

I love to work with mothers, spirituals women, 90s fans, glam queens, animal lovers and corporate gals. Why them? Because that is me. I am a stylist, love to take care of myself, help the animals, listen to 90s music and I myself have broke free finally from my corporate job.

Who are your tribe? They will look a little bit like you, but a few steps behind where you are today. Call them in. Market to them on Facebook, Twitter, Instagram etc. It's them that's gonna give you money from your services. If you want to be a coach then say you are one and start attracting your tribe in. Money will come easily when you decide on what you want. The problem with money is that if you are not clear on how to make it then it will not know how to come to you.

What do you want to sell to people? Is it books, programs, VIP days, coaching, products? Get clear on how the money will come to you and start market the thing you can sell today. There are tons of free social market places today and if you are just starting out use them. Facebook, Twitter, Instagram, Youtube, Periscope,

LinkedIn. Use them all if you want to or find 2-3 places you want to promote yourself. You can also guest blog if you want to or find podcast that you want to be interviewed on. It's all up to you and how you want it to happen.

But don't be too hard on yourself if things don't work out at first hand. For me it didn't. When I started my styling business I had no clients. I had to market myself and when people got to know me they bought my makeover days and personal shopper sessions. People has to know you before they buy from you. That's why you have to love yourself first and then you will attract the right clients that feel a connection with you.

After I did an interview once with a local paper I got a horrible client. She was not a perfect match. I had market myself to everyone. So of course she showed up. She thought that I was gonna fix her in just 5 hours and then she had her 2 month old baby with here and her mother on the side! I knew immediately that this was not a match. I should have walked away because this was not what I have signed up for. I hated this. And of course she wanted a refund on the day because she felt she didn't get to learn as much as she needed. Well it's hard when you have a screaming baby and a negative mother by your side...

Never again will I take a client on that is not serious about what she wants from me. We all learn about our mistakes and that's the good thing about bad things showing up in our lives.

You can decide on how you will make money, from who and how long it's gonna take. Set yourself up for fame and fortune online and be that shining star they have been waiting for. What do you want to be known for doing? The answer to that is that you can just start and do that know. What is stopping you? To believe in yourself, love yourself and get over your fears you have to journal about the woman you see yourself as. The one that is a killer chick. You are already an online star in your mind. See her first in your mind and describe her on paper how she would look like, how much money she is making, what she is known for, how she dresses, what her message is and how she impact others lives.

Be as specific you can, because money loves clarity. If something doesn't feel right, don't do it. This is your life, your business and you want that fame, fortune and be that online star. I know that people will be ready for you when you are ready to unleash yourself.

What kind of women do you see yourself as now? What do you have to be, do and have to become her with the recourses you already have? To really be her, you first have to see her and then live like her. I am an author. Am I an bestselling author? No. But I live like one. I write every single day, I market my books and I talk about me being an author. I live like I am a bestselling author. And I know I will be someday. I will never stop writing books, it's in my bones. Am I the best writer in the world? Hell no, but I could be if I really set my mind up for it. For now I write because that is some kind of therapy for me getting my message out there, and helping others go after their dreams.

What can you do today to be the online star you see yourself as? Do you want to be a famous business coach then you can definitive be that. Don't be like everyone else then. Go in another direction and sell results and sell what is your best advice on how they can be themselves and make money.

There are no other way because success and money and fame will come when you know who you are. If you don't know who you are and what your gifts are, then how can others buy from you then? They have to see you, know you and get attached to you before they buy from you.

It doesn't matter what you sell. Sell the things you love to do, create, be, show. You can do anything you like, but never loose faith in yourself and your capabilities to make your dreams happen. If you really want something and you love yourself no matter what, you will have it. Don't let your fear stop you. The truth is that other people are more concerned about themselves than thinking about what you do.

You have to make money if you want to live a life on your own terms. Money will come when you trust in yourself, believe that it's going to happen and when you can see it in your mind, then you can really feel it and then you will have it.

Focus on that money will give you freedom, a choice and you will feel fine with it. You deserve it. You can be that online star that we have been waiting for.

What are YOU waiting for?

CHAPTER 2: GET OVER YOUR FEARS!

The number 1 thing that is stopping people from getting what they want in life is fear. Fear of not being good enough, fear of not being brave enough, fear of what others might think of them. And the list goes on and on. What is your biggest fear right now? Write it down and face it. No matter what it is that you are resisting, facing your fears will give you a lighter and better life. There are no things that could pull you down if you love yourself and put love into all and get over your fears.

For many years I have been afraid that people would not like me. Strangers. What the hell. What was I thinking? Is it important if strangers like and love me? No. What is important in life and in business is to put yourself out there and claim that you are the next big thing coming up. You are that online star that could save others from falling into the trap of being like everyone else.

The world is sick and tired of copycats, try to be yourself for once and see what happens then. Who are you really? What is your biggest fears? Why are you afraid of putting yourself out there. The mafia will not go after you, and you don't sell drugs so what is it that is so scary that you have to pull those curtains down and hide behind your blanket? If you want success in life and in business, you have to wake up and be yourself. That's the only thing that will give you fame and fortune.

Don't be like everyone else out there trying to be seen and liked by all the others. With these bright and shiny objects that will give you endless of discovery calls and people will buy your 10k coaching package and love you forever. I don't think so. Those times are over. People understand when they are being fooled into something that is not real.

But if YOU stand up and tell them the truth how it really is, then you will be the online star that people have been waiting for. Stand for something, believe in something, be yourself and don't give a fuck about what they say. If you have to swear then do it, if you offends some then ok, and if you have to bleed for being yourself then JFDI (just fucking do it).

We are talking about you and your life right now. This is not a dress rehearsal where you get to perform and see if this is ok and will work out. Every single day you back out from yourself and your dreams, you back out from being you. From telling others how they also can live a life on their own term being themselves. Think how easy life will be when the only thing you have to think about is being you. It will come so natural and people will flock to you.

Some will not like you, but that is ok. You are not here to be liked by everybody. That is impossible. YOU don't like everybody do you? I know I don't. I don't hate on people but I stay away from the people I don't like. You have a choice and every single day you can choose to be you or choose to be like everyone else. Play the safe road that will give you endless of boring hours thinking about HOW your life could have turn out for the better or play for fun.

Are you not glad that now that you know this you can change it? Change your path. Life is running now every single day and you are playing your part. But are you playing safe or to your fullest? What is it that you want to do? Really want to accomplish in life? If you had all the time and the money you need what would you do with your life then? For me it's easy. I'm doing it. Write, speak, blog, make videos, coach people and kick your butt into action.

Are you now living your life just the way you want to or are you living in fear that you can't have, can't make it? Are you going all in or are you afraid that this is not gonna work. Well, it did not work being like everyone else so why don't you just try being yourself for once? «But I am myself» you say. No, you're not. Not that silly, honest, grumpy, crazy person that you know deep inside hate some things and love others thing. You tell me your are being you, but you have been hiding yourself from the rest of the world.

You know that crazy bitch that tells your husband what she really means. How she think life is. How silly she think her friends are trying to have a perfect life with big houses, cabin by the lake, 2.5 kids and be the perfect mother. Working long hours trying to look perfect on Facebook. You long to tell people about how you think they live their lives like a headless chicken running from errand to errand and trying to make their kids have a happy life going to soccer practice 4 times a week. Who are you kidding? Is he or she going to be the next Messi? I don't think so. Get the fuck up and live your life, not through your kids.

You don't dare to say that do you? Then you are not being yourself. You are NOT playing on your strengths and you can't take it when people don't like you. You say you are afraid of death. Let me tell you that it's not death that you should be afraid of. You should be afraid of yourself. You are the threat here, not all the others. You say you live a life you are happy with, are you really that happy after all?

Who is calling the shots in your life? You or you boss? Is it your kids schedule you're following the most or is it your happy schedule where you follow your dreams and make it a happy one? You will die someday, you know that? Then you will see that all your worries about what other people thought about you was just silly thoughts that held you back. But in reality they did not hold you back. You did it yourself!

You have the key to unlock your own life and live it, but you don't fucking care. You have enough on your plate with keeping up with all the brainless TV shows that are going on. How could you possible find time for yourself then?

And of course it's easy for the ones that already have made some money. They had their money fall into their lap. Of course they could do it. Not you. Pussycat!

You can't take it. You can't up level because you are a pussy. You want to have it your way and you believe that there is no other way. Your way or the highway. Silly silly girl.

When will you grow up and play with the other kids? The ones that go after their dreams? Play with the real people that don't give a shit about what some say about them. That's where you should be. Not on a soccer field bitching to the judge on how your kid is SO good and gonna be the next Beckham.

Your fears will stop you all day long, every day if you don't take care of it now. Shake them up. The world, your community, tell it like it is. Don't take things personal. You are not made of glass. You can hold it together. Let them hear it. The truth and nothing but the truth. But you are not that brave are you? Then you're not being yourself. You say you are but you're not. You are just like all the rest. Trying to please everyone and saying the perfect things to the polish perfect barbie dolls. The ones that are just like you. Trying to be perfect. Trying to be liked by others.

Get the fuck up and get over yourself. You are THAT SPECIAL. If someone told you another story then they can fuck themselves. You are special because you are being YOU. If you really want to.

Take it. Grab it. The negative one, the positive part of you. Play on all your strengths and be yourself. Really be yourself, because now you are only playing a part that doesn't fit in. You are playing small. If you really want to be the next online star then get over your fears and tell it like it is. Tell them how life is and how you can help them change it to the better. Why are you trying if you're not REALLY trying? Then I would rather suggest you go back to a safe job and kill yourself with boring TV shows.

I want to shake you up. Wake you up. I have woken up myself from sleep and its time for me to unleash myself being me. There are no one like me or like you. If you really go for it, all in then you gonna make it. How I know? All the others out there give up or are fake.

If you are the one that tells the truth and be 100% yourself and authentic, of course you're gonna make it. Be in love with yourself, get over your fears and be you. That is the receipt for success. No matter what you want to become in this world you can make it. If you have a dream in your heart you feel is too big to come true then it's there for a reason.

You will be the next online star if you go after it, claim it. I'm here. Look out world, I'm coming. But fear will stop you. People will think you are crazy, too much, too loud, too you. But that's the price for being yourself. Would you rather be someone else? Don't be a pussy and don't take the fame and fortune that is right in front of you. It's there. It's yours. You can have it. But not if you are a copycat.

They will notice you if you copy them. Unleash yourself from your fears and just let it out. All the silliness you have inside of you. All the craziness that has been holding you back and let it out into the world. We need it. I know I do. I love authentic people. The other polished ones are great to look at, but they are not being themselves. Some may be. But for the rest. Nada.

So how can you today get over your biggest fears? Who do you have to be to get over it? What do you have to do? If you're afraid of being seen then you have to put yourself out there. If you are afraid of speaking the truth about a topic, then that is what you have to do. And if you fear living a life chained to a 9-5 job then you better start working on your dreams baby. You got one life. It's on right now. The show will always go on, with you in it or not. No matter what others might think of you, there are only one person that can change your life and we both know who that is? Not me. This book will kick you in the butt and give you motivation to be that next online star out there.

Play safe and kill your dreams or play bold and brave and have success. Your choice. What's it gonna be honey?

CHAPTER 3: BUILD A STRONG MINDSET

Everything you want to have you must see in your mind before it's happening on the outside. If you today don't have the results you wish for, then it's only because you don't have a strong enough mindset. Before I was very insecure about myself and did not dare to put myself in front of other people. That was why no one could buy from me. They could not see me because I was hiding and therefor they could not buy from me. I was broke.

Now today I market myself everyday and I'm proud that I'm an author and have written 7 books and on my way to my eight book. I see it in my mind the things I want. But when it comes to money you have to program yourself and take an upgrade. Think of your brain like a computer, once in a while you have to upgrade that computer so it works better and so is it for you. You have to upgrade you thoughts and beliefs about yourself and about money.

It's hard to do this but you have to build it up if you want to learn to think like a millionaire. They have very strong mindset and think positive about themselves and about money. What did your parents say about money when you grew up as a little girl? Was it the root of all evil? That wealthy people was unhappy. That you can't build a business on your dreams and make money doing what you love? If this was what you were taught then you can see why you are not making any money today in your business.

You have to find new beliefs and say them to yourself everyday, and see them and feel them. Then you can change the way you think about money and about yourself. If you can't see yourself as the next online star out there then it's gonna be hard to be that kind of women. Everything you really want you have to see in your mind and feel it before it's happening. It's a minds game to make it in the online community. You are gifted, beautiful and you can have all the success you want, but you have to build a strong mindset around you and money.

My mindset now is pretty strong. People tell me that all the time and I can say that this has not been an easy walk in the park. I have been journaling every morning, said out loud affirmations 3 times a day, listen to inspiring podcast, youtube videos and read a ton of money books. I have set my mind up for success but I have to keep going or I will loose it. Its like going to the gym. You will never be done, if you want to keep up what you have accomplished you have to keep doing the job.

Same goes for mindset. But it will be easier when times goes by. This will be like taking a breath. You don't think about it, you just do it. When you have that strong mind, all you have to do is program yourself into new beliefs you would like to see happening and then all your dreams can come true.

I think it's wonderful to know that I myself have the power in me to change just the way I like to. That I don't have to start on the outside but first program my mind, think about it, feel it in my bones, take action on it and then the results will appear. And if the results are not like I wanted them to be, then I know that it has nothing to do about my actions and the outer things, it's always in my programmed mind, my thoughts and my feelings. Then I go back and change them for the better.

I can run my world just the way I want to and so can you. You have this power within you to change your life, your thoughts and you feelings. When bad thing happens to you, know that your reaction to it will give you the outcome you believe will happen. Be positive and know that everything happens for a reason. You can handle whatever comes your way.

A strong mindset will give you an invisible force that many don't know about. You will use it to your best in life and in business and you know that if you're not that online start yet, you will be. When you change your thoughts about yourself you can make it.

When you read inspiring books, which I think you should do every day, then pick some that lifts your mind and talks about how to think not how to act. The acting process is not the first thing that must be on your mind. You will take action on behalf of the beliefs, thoughts and feelings that you have. So you can actually take wrong action because on how you think and feel. That's why the action step is not the most important one to focus on.

You must focus more on your mindset than anything else if you want the outcome to be that online star you deserve to be. You deserve the best that you can have and you are special. You are being you. But believe in yourself and build your mind strong before you give up on yourself. The action you have taken up until now, has it been aligned with your passion and purpose? If not then maybe that's why you don't have the success you want.

The way you feel and think about yourself, and life in general, will give you the life you have today! Yes, the life you have today is created on the things you say to yourself in your mind every single day. Are you kind to yourself or do you bitch to yourself about not being good enough and smart enough? Talk gently to yourself and push when it is needed. Many women are so afraid that if they don't take action and push themselves they will not succeed. But that is the wrong way of thinking about it.

If you really want success in business and in life, you have to fix your programming. That is the first and most important task you have to do. Start today. What you hear will disappear so you have to see it in your mind and write it down on paper the things you would like see happening. Also write down your new beliefs about money. Get rid of the ones that your parents told you. Don't blame them, it was passed from their parents to them.

Now that you know that you can change your thoughts about yourself and then change your actions, you will have success in business and in the online market place. You will come up with new ideas on how you would do things different from all the others out there. Maybe it's not about competing but it's about collaborations? And maybe it's not about following a set of rules but about letting it all go and work from a place of joy.

Who knows how your path is gonna look like? Very different to mine I guess. But one thing I know, is that if you never give up, you will have success. But you don't have to make it so hard on yourself.

When you figure it out then success, money and fame will flow to you easily. You will have lot's of money and people will ask you how you did it. You can't answer that because it just happened in a blink of an eye. Money and fame will come your way when you believe it, see it, claim it and take action on it. But if your action step is the first thing in your mind, you will never get there.

Yes, you can have some kind of success doing certain things, but I have noticed that the majority of people don't follow programs, and advice from others. They fall of the wagon after 2 weeks and then they are back in the loophole again. That is because they are following other peoples steps and paths. They are not fixing their mindset before they take action. So I suggest that if you are thinking about buying another online course then let it be a mindset one. All the others will not give you the success you want if you don't have a strong mindset already.

I know it because I have tried it. Nothing worked for me before my mindset was built up on success. When you have a strong mind you will take action and call the right people, fear will go away, you will say yes to things you really want to do and say no to things that feels wrong. You will be so aligned and work, talk, act like a millionaire that money, fame and fortune will flow to you.

You have it in you. Just unleash yourself and the things you want to believe in. You have the power inside of you.

When I first started out in my business I had a very low self-esteem and a weak mindset. I thought that I was not good enough, that no one was gonna buy from me and that I did a crappy job. It was all in my mind and it reflected out on the people I worked with. I was so anxious at a time that I just wanted to quit my job as a stylist because I thought that others was way better than me. But that was not true. And all the others was working and building their mindset towards getting more clients and more customers. I was busy talking down on myself.

To put yourself out there is not easy, but when you work on your mindset it will be so much easier. You will not think so much about what other people say about you. You just do the things that feels right for you. What is it that you really want to see happening with your online business right now? It can happen. But that kind of women you see in your mind, how does she think about herself? Talk to herself? Act? What kind of promoting does she do? Who does she reach out to that she wants to work with? What does she say about money?

Tear yourself down before you build it up again. You have to be really honest about how you think and feel about yourself. You are the key to your happiness and your online fame. If you want to be that star on stage then you have to put up with negative people, naysayers, critics etc. Could that be why you don't are that online star yet? That you think that if I get really well known then some people will not like me for who I am? Guess what. Some don't like you today because of the person you are. That's their problem, not yours.

Get over yourself and build a strong mindset that will give you fame, fortune and all the things you want in life. You have to really be there to get it. It's not the other way around. Start with your programs in your head and take an upgrade on how you think about yourself. Then you will get the outcome you crave. You will not take wrong action. And if the outcome doesn't work then you have to take another upgrade. That's the thing for computers and thats the same thing for you and your brain.

Build a strong mindset and set yourself up for success. This is a very important chapter so go back and read it over and over until you get it. You have to get this before you get all the other things in this book.

CHAPTER 4: SHINE LIKE A STAR!

You got to shine like a star. A star that means it. You want to be so freaking happy about your life that no one could rock you out from your dream. You could sit there like I do now and write a book and the whole world could fall apart, but you would not notice it. You would not notice them because you are so busy living your life and shine like the star you know you are. You have it in you and you have been holding it back for so long and now it's time to just unleash you. Unleash that fucking crazy bitch that shines like a star and knows it. They see you. They can't believe that you are so obsessed with life and with yourself.

They see you as that crazy selfish bitch that thinks she has it all. And you do have it all. You do. You can feel it in your bones and in your heart. It fills your mind all day long and it will never go away. You have it in you to really become more than you could possible dream about. Maybe you now only dream about a 6 figure business when the reality is that you could have a billion business if you set your mind up for it.

You dream to small, but in your mind you know that you can have it all. The really big bucks. Not because you need it. You are more than happy with just living your life just the way you like on your own. Doing the things that other people said to you that is impossible. You're living it right now. They see you but they will never get you. You can try to tell them how to live a life in alignment but you will never get them to change no matter what.

You are here to shine the light upon them that need it the most. The women who lives life in scarcity that this is it. This is her life. This is all there is to it. You are here for her to tell her that she can also have it all. The life, fame, fortune and be her own online star. Never in life has it been easier to start a business and make money from all around the world. We are no longer trapped to a 9-5 job we hate. I am over that now. There is no other option than living life from your heart and doing the things you are put here on earth to do.

You are not here to only pay bills and die. You have a purpose that is bigger than life and I believe that we all have some messages we are here to tell. I think that I am here to wake people up from their sleep. Life is passing by day by day and are they living life to the fullest? Yes, you can create success from and outer place. Doing more work, promoting more, following the steps but I don't think you can create fame and be that online star you long for if you do it from the wrong kind of service.

I believe that you have to create it from within yourself. The craziness that you don't talk to people about, but you long to unleash. You have to shine like a star. Shine like yourself. Create it around you. In the way you dress, talk, walk, feel. Feel it inside of you that you have it. Everything.

You can dress just the way you like. If you want to look polished then do that. If you want to dress in gym gear then go for it. It's always up to you. I love wearing gold and silver sparkling clothes and I love ripped up jeans and leather boots and jackets. I am me. I shine like me.

I don't try to be anyone else but myself. Who are you here to please? You are here to please yourself and no one else. And think about this. Put all your gifts together in an outstanding brand that is YOU. No one can copy being you. They can try but they could only reach you to your knees. You are you in all your craziness, all your beliefs, the way you dress, talk, act and the way you are to other people. If you are that crazy and kind one that does things just the way she like it straight from the heart, then no one could ever compete with you. And the best thing is that your tribe, your flock, will come to you. You call on them and they will come to you. You will be the leader, the shining star up there on stage and it will all be worth it. The struggles you have been through and all your sleepless nights when money did not come your way.

Money will flow to you when you shine like a star. That's the big secret to fame. When you got fame then money loves it. It will come. But you want fame in the right way by being yourself and looking just the way you are. You work from your heart and talk from your heart. You are making money just by being you. Dosen't that sound nice?

You know the IT girls they really has it together. But first no one notices them. But small things in their everyday life get notices and then when the breakthrough came it came so fast that it almost happen overnight. But it was not overnight. It was daily action day by day. Maybe it was intentional or maybe not.

The clue is that if you take everyday action upon being yourself and talking and acting in a way that is authentic, then you will shine like a star. You are actually there today. In your life who sees you as that star? Don't say no one because if you have kids then they will adore you, your husband, your mother, father, sister, friends, clients. For someone in your life YOU are the star. They look to you and believe in you. They see you and want to have what you have. They love you.

Love yourself for being just the way you are and don't let no one tell you otherwise. You are more than capable to do all the things you dream about. If you dream it, you can achieve it. Take action everyday and put yourself out there, even if they don't see you, comment on your blogpost, like what you got today. There will always always always be someone that like what you have to say.

When you are so raw and authentic and talk in a way that no one else dare to, then you will call them in. Call in your tribe and shine like the star you already are. If you are authentic in everything you do you can't go wrong in life. Buy the clothes you like, not what all the others do. Dress in a way that you feel comfortable with and give a fuck about what all the others out there tells you to dress like. Are you a puppet? No, I don't think so.

Life is passing by so quickly that you can't do more of the unauthentic shit anymore. It's all gone and you have to believe a little bit more in yourself that you are capable to make it. Be an online star. Not for the sake of it, hell no. Because you have an important message to put out there. I'm not talking about how you dress when I say online star. I talk about the way you talk, write, act, uplift people, your honesty, but if you want to put a nice dress on doing it, then go ahead.

I would like to see more women talk deep down from their heart about things they see missing in the online industry. There are many coaches out there, but not many authentic ones. Be her. That one that tells it like it is and shine like a star because she owns it. She knows that she must be here and now and stand up for every women out there who is struggling with things she has been through.

No matter how hard life hits you in the face you have to pick yourself up time and after time. And if you don't get what you want you have to change the way you see yourself as. It always comes down to your mindset and what you believe can happen. Everything you believe can come true if you really see it and feel it. Ignore debt, ignore that you have no clients, ignore lack, ignore the naysayers. Set your mindset so high on vibration that no one can rock it. There are no one out there who could take away from you how you see yourself. I'm not talking about in a vain way. I talk about that you have to believe in yourself and your capabilities that you have it in you to become a millionaire or whatever else you see yourself as.

You always have the key to your own destiny and your success. I want it all. The fame, the fortune, become a bestselling author, work with cruelty free companies, live a life where I can travel more, lots of money. Give money to charity, buy my mother an apartment close by, buy a nice car. I am so grateful for where I am today. I have what I want but I could always go for more. That's why I work every single day on my dreams. If I want to be a best selling author I have to write and write and contact publishers.

I now have 3 books published in English on Amazon and this will be my fourth one. I will never stop writing. I don't know how many books I have to write to really get there, but I know one thing.

I will never give up on my dreams just because they aren't happening in the timeframe I would like to. I could say I have some sort of fame online being the online stylist for female entrepreneur, but that is not my ultimate goal. I want to shake the world up and tell women to go out and live life on their terms and making money just by being you.

Online stars have some kind of things in common. They have a big audience, lots of clients, make money and look fab. But can you really know if they got it together? No. They are only humans just like you and me. If you meet them in real life some of them are not that kind and special.

But the ones that are really authentic love their clients and could go to have wine with them and be like friends. It's all up to you how you want it. You have to be kind to everyone because they deserve it. They will look up to you and feel a connection so don't push them away. You could always say no in a kind way. Who knows what life will bring you. You're better of if you have been nice to people if you have to ask them a favor.

Be that nice, kind, crazy one with a big heart and who believes just as much in her clients as she does in herself. They want to be like you, look like you, have what you have. Don't take that dream away from them if you act like a diva. Of course you can do whatever you like, but that is my opinion on how the online community works.

Shine like a star and be yourself. The world doesn't need you to be polished. The world would like you to tell it like it is and that you are yourself in anyway you can. In this way you show them that they can also be like that. People buy from people. Remember that.

I want to see you glow. Go out now and take your fame. You deserve it.

CHAPTER 5: BE FUCKING AWESOME!

If you really want to shake the world then you have to be fucking awesome. You can be one that gives a fuck about what other thinks about you, but you give and give and give people more than they expect from you. Then you will be freaking awesome. No one does it. They only give you 5% of the things they really have and then they charge you big bucks to give you the really cool stuff.

Don't be like them, just be you and give more than they expect. You can have it all if you just go all in with all your advice and gifts and don't hold yourself back. If you give them the really cool shit they don't expect, then you are the queen online. There are no easy path to be the online star if you are in it to just make money. But I know that you are in it to win it and then you can really just let it all out and give of yourself. Give so much that they drop their mouth and can't believe how much you give for free. Don't hold it back, because if you give of yourself that good shit they will definitive give their money to work with you.

You have it all going on when you claim to be the next online star. All you have to be is to be fucking awesome and then go out and claim that you know it all, you know your shit and the things that you are good at. I know that many coaches tells you that you should not give too much, but I personal think that it's a wrong way to try to get noticed for all your gifts.

When you don't feel like giving of yourself, you know someday when it all feel like shit, then is actually the day you should talk about how you feel and tell them the honest truth about yourself. No one does it. They only talk about when they have good things happening in their life. But people will love to hear that you are only human and that life can be hard sometimes.

Why are not people awesome?

They don't claim it. They play small in their own life. What the fuck? It's their life but they play small when they could go out and change other peoples life. Don't be like them. Be like you and be awesome. Be so amazing that the people you impact will talk about you to their friends, family and they will love you so much that they will send you an email and thank you that you have changed their life.

That is to make an impact. That is to change peoples life.

The other fluff and «how to» steps are not interesting at all. Yes, people love to read about it but they will never take time to implement it. Think about it yourself, do you implement the «how to» steps you read about? I know I don't.

We all live busy lives and want to have success and make money doing what we love. Yes, we do and if you read this book and you don't feel the same way then this book is wrong for you. If you are only in it to read inspiring stuff then you can find another book. I want you to be fucking awesome and claim that you are. Not in a vanity way, but just because you know that you are going after your dreams and you want to live a life that few people can because they can't take the pain it is to go after their dreams. This is not a walk in the park. This is life and it's not supposed to be that easy to really be clear on what you want in life. If it was easy, everyone else would have done it. They don't. Because they love to live comfortable lives AND bitch about people that go after their dreams and make money doing it.

I am sick and tired of you playing small. Just unleash yourself and start talking about the stuff that THEY don't dare to.

You have to be awesome to live a life where you mean something to others. If you don't feel it in your bones that this is it, then just go away and live your comfortable life. But then give yourself permission to stop dreaming about how life could be.

Life can be easy if you want it to be easy. You have to be the one that take charge over you life and stop dreaming about how you want it to be. Start being the person you want to be. You don't have to ask for permission to anyone for how you can talk, act, be. This is your life and you can be awesome if you want to. Do you want to be awesome? Then claim it and just be it. Now!

I know it can be hard to think of yourself as awesome when you don't have so many clients on your list, and money is not showing up in your business. But the only thing you have to do is to show up every single day and be you. Talk about what you believe in, be the one who tells the truth and claim that you are on your way for something big.

The thing you want to see happening in your life will come true when you see yourself there. Be there now. Not in a vanity way, but feel it in your heart. Stop checking your account to see if money is coming your way. Stop talking bad about yourself and don't talk about that you have no clients. They will show up when you say that you are finished playing small in your life, in other peoples life.

You are awesome because you try. Think about all the people that don't try it. They only talk about how they want their life to be. They are unhappy about their life, but they never take action on the things they don't like. They think that they don't have a saying in life, that life only happens TO them. Not that they can take charge of the things that HAPPENS to them.

You know that you can get caught up in the busy life and how people bitch about how wrong life is. There is nothing we can change in life, other than changing ourselves. You can show them how to change but you can't change them. They have to take it and claim it all by themselves.

So if you are fucking awesome then people will see that and want to be like you and try to follow you around. They will ask you how you can be so lucky all the time and have all your shit together, but you know deep down that this is an inside job. You have been through hell and back, but never given up on your dreams and your life.

Are you not happy that you can call the shots in your life and live it according to your heart? That is the only way to be you. To be awesome. You are awesome when you help people. When you give your all. When you play on your strengths. When you are yourself. You have only one life and you know that you have to live it now. We only got this life and that's why you have to be awesome every single day. Don't try to be like everyone else. Be you.

Awesome people give more. Talk positive about life. Glow. Look nice. Are beautiful. They give more than they ask for. They know that they can have it all and are not afraid to go out and take it.

They want others to have the same. They want to give more to others, but they also know that they are worthy of making money from their gifts. They are not dreading Mondays, they love Mondays. They love life. Life is easy for the fucking awesome people. Life is good. And they know it every single day. It's never about how much money, it's always about how much freedom they have. With money comes freedom so don't talk negative about money. You have to have money if you want freedom and live a life on your own terms.

What do you do today to be you? To be fucking awesome? Think about how the people you look up to seems to be so awesome. What is it that they do? Talk about? Look like? The way they dress, act, speak?

Don't copy them, but get inspired about them and be you and just as awesome as they are. Do you really want it? The fame, fortune, money and success? Then you have to get over yourself and

being afraid about what others think about you and talk about you behind your back.

There are no way in between. You have to be comfortable with being uncomfortable.

Life is supposed to be live the way you want it to be, but then you have to bleed for it. Just a while until you really get it. You get that you are capable to have it all and be awesome when you are being true to yourself?

Why are you so special you ask? You are special because you claim it. You have a dream and you go after it. How many people do that? And then when it dosen't work out, you don't give up. How many people give up? And then when you have to go back to a part time job and work on your dreams on the side, you do that. Or you find a way it can work out.

You will never ever give up on yourself and the belief that you are the new online star that is gonna shake the world. You could have given the most in your local business, but you know that you are meant for so much more. You are the online star. I know you are. Believe in yourself and know that you are capable to so much more than you could ever image.

You are not a whiny bitch that does things to hurt other people. Like the ones that talk behind other women's back. Talk to yourself in the way you want others to talk to you. Don't think for a second that you are not good enough. I know that bitches will come and talk you down, let you know that you are not good enough and can't make it. Fuck them.

You can be whatever you would like to be. You have it in you. Trust in yourself and believe that you can have it. The fame, fortune and the money to create a freedom where you call the shots in your life. You believe you can have it and then you can. It's that easy. Stop being caught upon the hard things in life. Claim that life is easy, talk good to people and prepare for the best to come. Life is meant to be happy and lived to the fullest. Of course the world needs you. The world need another online star that will take it, claim it and belive she can have it.

I'm gonna be up there with you. Applaud you and tell all the others about you. I know you got it, just show them. Show them that you have what it takes and just take it and be yourself.

You are the next online star. Yes, you are!

CHAPTER 6: LET SELLING BE EASY

Y ou know that you got it and you want to have lots of
clients coming your way. But that dosen't mean that
you're gonna sell easy. You have to promote yourself and
sell what you got. Actually you have to promote and always be
selling. When you are out there online and be yourself, then you
have to ask for the sale, promote what you got or else no one is
gonna buy from you.

When you are really sold on your stuff then you will sell easy and
fast. You have to first be true to yourself and look at what you got
now. Is there anything on your sales page that you don't like and
not feel aligned with the person you see yourself as? If the answer
is yes then get rid of it. Make new offers that are so clear on who
they are meant for that they will sell like hot cakes.

You don't have to feel that selling is hard. Selling is easy when you
know your products so well and you know what kind of people
you want to sell to. Then the sales process will be easy. You don't
have to sell or make anything in your business that dosen't feel
right for you. If you have to break your business and start all over
again, then do it. It will be worth it when you sell from your heart.
Then you will have lots of clients and your true self will shine
through.

The sales process should not be like pulling teeth out of people, you have to be comfortable with what you got and then sell it like hot cakes. And if it dosent work the first time, then you have to tweak it a bit and try again. Be so clear that people know if this is for them or not. Don't try to sell to everybody, you are not here for everyone. You are her for your tribe.

This was a huge mistake I did in the beginning of my styling business. I tried to sell my makeover days to every woman out there. Young girls, old ladies, grannies. I market it to men so they could buy it to their partners, to daughters, to a bunch of people. I was not clear on who my ideal clients was so it was hard to sell it to someone.

I think you have hear it before that you have to be clear on your tribe. But the thing you do now as an online star is to call them in. Tell them how they are, what they like and why they will benefit from your service or products, and then you have to figure out where they hang out. Hang around with them and tell them what you got to offer.

If you want to write a book and sell you can bet that other people who write books will buy from you. Hang around them. And if you want to help other coaches to skyrocket their business, then you have to hang around new coaches who needs your help. Call them inn and tell them how you can help.

Selling is easy when you know:

1. What you sell
2. Who you sell it to
3. How they can benefit from your service or product

So can you answer these 3 questions easy? If not then you have to try to make them easy. Be sold on yourself and know that you got something special that the other ones don't have. Many days you will not feel like selling yourself, and the motivation will be long gone. Then you have to try to motivate yourself into asking yourself why you started. Your business should not feel like a pain in the ass. It should feel like freedom and that you are creating something bigger than yourself. You are in it to win it and then you have to make the sales process easy.

What can you do today to make your sales process easier? Do you have a free opt in on your website? If not, then create it. Let it be so awesome that people could not avoid to see it and sign up. And when they sign up, let them receive 2-3 emails after where you give them even more great stuff they will love. Then you ask them to buy something from you. Maybe an ebook, coaching with you or an online course. If you have given them something they really love they will buy from you. If not then don't cry.

You just have to figure out if you where clear enough on what you sell, if they are the right people and how they can benefit from it. It's that easy but we women make is pretty hard. We think that we are not good enough and the shit we sell are not great. That's bullshit. Get clear on your products and service and then sell it to the right people. They will love it when they understand it.

I know that I buy from people that give me so much free content that I can't say no to their offers. And sometimes I feel a connection, they tell a story I can relate to and how they got through it. Then I buy from them. My clients often buy from me because I am authentic and tell it like it is. But it has not been like that from the beginning. In the beginning of my Norwegian online business I made a blog schedule where I had written down 52 titles on blog post I was gonna write. I felt ok in the beginning of it, but after a while I felt bored. The people did not respond to it either so I was not writing from my heart and on topics that I loved.

I felt not ok. I felt trapped in an online business I did not love. I created online course after online course and many of them sold well. But when I look back now it was never created from my heart. This was not was I was meant to do with my life.

I knew that my ultimate goal was to have an English online

business so I could find my tribe and impact more people. I think actually I sabotage my business because I wanted it so much to write books in English and have my coaching business.

Life will give you lemons and hard kicks in the butt. You have to sell easy. Sell your services like you sell to your kids, husband. Be you in an authentic way. People love when others tell the whole truth and nothing but the truth. If you have never tried to be yourself in selling then you are in for a treat. But you have to really feel it in your bones that you are yourself. Don't think about what will sell. Be honest about who you are, why you sell it and how they can benefit from it. Tell them that you don't work with everybody but you work with this kind of people. Then list the things you see in them that you would like your ideal clients to have.

The more clear you are about what you sell, why you sell it and who you sell to, the easier your sales process will be. Then you don't have to think about it on a strategic way what your next offer is gonna be. Then you create from your heart and give them your best stuff. The stuff that you need when you were in their shoes. They need mindset work, money stuff, how to create from the heart, how to be authentic, how to do thing that comes easy for you but not for them.

You can offer them whatever you feel you can help them with. Do it all with love and from your heart. I can honestly say that I have broken down my business many times. Now I break it apart again. I just want to write and coach other women into finding their true calling. I don't want to style anymore. Styling and makeup is ok but that is not what is closest to my heart. That is not my calling. What is your calling? What do you feel deep down you are here to do?

Whatever it is you can do it. When I wanted to become a stylist I did it. When I wanted to become an author, I did it. When I want my business to take another direction, I do it. I don't ask for permission anymore to follow my heart. You know you have it in you and you are the next online star. You can work as much as you like and as little as you like. The world is right there in front of you. The only thing you have to do is to go out there and take it. Start on your dreams and shine like a star.

I have a calling and then when I want to sell it I sell easy. If you have to change all your business pages and your about page then do it. But you don't have to wait until you sell your next program. You can sell it today. First you write your amazing sales page, then you market it and set an earlybird price. Give it a week and then you set the price higher. If no one buys it then tweak it a bit and ask yourself if you where clear enough? If not, then do it over again.

I have made many programs that did not sell. I felt ashamed of myself, that I was not good enough and that I was a failure. But I picked myself up again and then created another thing. You got to create from your heart. Your art will never come from your head. You can be strategic about services and products, but that will never last you in the end. You have bought this book to really shine like yourself. You are not out here on earth to be like all the rest out there. You are here to make an impact on a bigger scale. Then you have to make your sales process easy so you don't give up to fast.

I read a lot of sales books also to learn new stuff. I feel that I can always learn more and be better in what I do. If you are in business you have to manage to sell your stuff. Make it easy for yourself and let the creating process be the one you set most time aside to.

Would it not be fun if your service and stuff sold easy. That at least 10 people signed up on all your new things every time? It can be that way. The more you create, the more you sell. The more you sell the more you can be yourself and live a life in freedom where you call the shots in your life.

Life and business is supposed to be easy. And the sales process is very easy for the ones who are sold on themselves and knows how they can help. Get crystal clear about what you do and for who you do it. Then market like you mean it.

You should not be ashamed about yourself and that you have a business. Let them know about you all your friends, family, old colleagues etc. People often get inspired if you open up and talk about what you do. If they are not interested, their loss.

But sell easy, all day and everyday. Then you will have a business that will blossom, be authentic and you will love to get out of bed in the morning. Let yourself be that person you dream about. If it is a coach then coach people. Start for free. If you want to be an author then write and sell your books on Amazon. You can make it easy or hard. What do you choose?

CHAPTER 7: GET YOUR MESSAGE OUT THERE

You have to get your message out there every single day. People have to know about your and all your amazing things you have created. It doesn't matter if you are a coach, a stylist, author, a new business owner. The things that matters is you, and you have to tell people about it. You must do that every day. I take some time off on Sundays and Saturdays, but my message is always the same. I know that you can have it all and live a life on your own terms.

This weekend I have been in a wedding in beautiful Lofoten in Norway. There I met a lot of people telling about what they did for a living. Everyone was so impressed by me and my speech to the bride. I did it in a fun an inspiring way that I knew people would like. I want people to get inspired by me, my way and my life. I have been trapped to long in a corporate world where all that matters is numbers and that you are on time to do the work that I feel doesn't matter to anyone.

I know that if you have some gifts inside of you it could be a book, an online course or a product, you have something special that people needs. You then have to believe in yourself and get your true message out there every day.

There are so many women out there trying to copy other with their nice website, same approach that you can earn 6 figures in only 6 weeks etc. I think that could be a scam an of course THEY can make 6 fig if they tell you that because you buy from them when the real truth is that they have not made it before until now.

I believe that we should speak our real truth to people and tell all about how our path has been. Our message is important in this world. If someone else has the same message that only means that you got it. You really got it but you have to make it your own way. Say it with your words. You can be whoever you want to be and act the way you like. Don't let anyone else dictate your pathway to freedom. We're all in this to win it so why shouldn't we make ways for other people?

I think that if we stand together as one we stand taller and stronger. If you find someone out there with the same message as you reach out to them and be strong together.

When I see somebody that has the same message that I have I will follow them and back them up on that message.There can never be any competition if you sell yourself and your real truth. The things that you have inside of your will no one else tell the same way as you can.There can never be another you. So act on it and sell your message every single day.

Some of my coaching clients think that it is so hard to speak the truth every day when they don't have the success and money right now. They feel like a fraud. I tell them to write things for themselves that they feel they need. Because if you write from your heart there will always be someone else who feels the same as you do. They need to hear it and they will start to follow you. We all have started with one clients, one on our list and it will always we one thing. The first book, your first live event, your first money. The clue is to always be true to your message deep inside of you because then all things in your business will explode when you put the real you in front of people.

I think that people are sick and tired of women who acts in one way online and are like another person when they meet them in real life. Ask yourself how can you be more authentic in your business? What is it that you want to tell people about life? What kind of gift is so easy for you to do but you know that others struggles with them? That's you pinpoint and that's where you money will come from.

I love reading inspiring books and can never get enough of them. That's why I have decided on writing this as my first book in many and publish it myself on amazon. What's your big dream now that you put of doing?

First when I started my English business I thought that my English was not good enough. That people will not understand me, but that was just myself sabotaging my international success. To have really success as an online business women you have to put yourself out there with your message every day. You have no time to waste on things and thoughts that doesn't matter in the end. The end will come sooner or later and then I think that you would have been sorry that you didn't try.

If you give it a try and do everything from your heart where can you be 6 months from now? I know that I can have a million dollar business in 6 months from now. I can write 20 books in that time if I set my mind up to it. I could grow my list super fast and act on things immediately. I have no time to waste. I'm in it to win it. I want to live a life on my terms and then I have to just do the f.... work every day.

I have no time to loose. I have said goodbye to my successful Norwegian business because this is it. My ultimate goal is to live life on my terms the laptop life and working with client all around the world.

If you think that it's hard to find out what your message is then you can look at things that inspire you. I can see that the things I read about, I feel is important and I want to talk and write about that all the time. We have no time to waste that's why we have to work on our message every day. You can do it the way that feels right for you. Write a blog post, make a video on youtube, periscope, live google hang out, webinar etc. It's all up to you as long as you do the work. That's all that matters.

Sometimes you don't feel like doing anything. I know that and it happens to me also, but the clue is then to just f.... do it anyway. I didn't feel like writing a new chapter on my book this morning but I knew that if I didn't do it I will feel so much worse afterwords. Now I'm all in and feel the flow in my writing. Just act on the thing that is a must everyday and all thing will fall into place. Your message is super important to get out there every day.

If just 1 person get it then hurray, you did something right. You don't have to feel bad if you just started out and no one is reading your blog, newsletter etc. Be happy about the ones that opens your newsletter, reach out to you and know that you have touch their heart in some way. That's your tribe, that's the people you want to follow you.

I feel bad about leaving my Norwegian clients behind but I know that I have millions to reach and then I can't waste more time writing to so few people in a language that just a small population understand.

The ones that liked my Norwegian site can come and join my English one. They will love to be a part of my new journey to freedom. You can't let something stop you from getting your message out there. There is no other way to go. It's all up to you to get your message across to the right people. Hang around with people that thinks and act like you. Be the 1% and be happy with that. I sometimes feel like a freak and that nobody understands me, but then I turn to those people who actually understand me.

You could create your own groups online or you can find a local entrepreneur group who can support you. But the only one that you have to confirm to is yourself. Nobody else knows how you feel and think. They can't understand your path to freedom because they are not on it. And if people around you don't seek freedom why should you surround yourself with them? They will never understand you. They are so in the box that they would rather die than getting out into the real world trying to make a living for themselves.

You got it in you and you know what to do with your life. You have a voice and people wants to listen to you, follow you and get inspired by you. Never rob them of what your got because you don't know how you can get your message out there. Scream it from the rooftop if you have to. I don't care about what other people think about me anymore. I just love being myself and help other women find their true voice and path to freedom.

I have always played it safe in life and in my career. I thought that when I earned a good salary I would be happy and satisfied and that was it. But that day came when I have reached my goal. I was not happy because I haven't listen to my heart. The voice inside that always has said to me that «Camilla you can become what you set you mind up to». I have always believed in myself and that I was capable to do all the things I dreamt about.

I have been a dreamer for so long as I can remember and a big part of my heart has always been to travel the world, live location free and visit big cities like Paris, London, Milan and NY. I love the energy in the big cities but I also want to go to destinations like Bali, LA and Hawaii. I can understand tourist who comes to Norway and fall in love with the nature, mountains and the ocean. I love living near the ocean and listen to the sound of sea gulls.

I think that you have to live your dream life now. Be a big part of the things you say you want in life and just act like you have it now. Decide that it's gonna be yours. If you really want it you got to chase after it and never give up.

I'm in it to win it and will never go back to a safe and steady life as I had before. It's now I love my life. It's now I live and get my message across to people. This is it. Start living yours too.

What is one thing you can do today to get your message to other people? What do you like most of writing, talking, filming etc. Find you way and make it a must to act on it every single day. Let people know about you so they can buy from you and you can help them become their best version in this world. Start now. Today!

CHAPTER 8: START WITH WHY

Are you crystal clear about why you do what you do? If not then you have to find out really fast. Be sold on yourself so that other people will be sold on you. Your message is probably why you do what you do. If your why is to have more freedom, be your own boss and make a difference in this world, then talk about it all the time. Do it in your daily blogs, your newsletter and in your sales pages. This is why people buy from you and why they will feel connected to you.

Your «why» will also help you at times when you feel not doing your daily work and when nothing feels right. When you have no customers and no one is buying your shit. Then you have to ask yourself why you started and who your are here for. If you're only in it to make money then I can tell you this will be a long and boring task. You have to feel passion and purpose behind your goals.

Even if your goal is to make 1 million dollar in your business, there will be a «why» behind. My why is that I want more freedom, be my own boss and mean something to other women who know they have a calling but don't know how to get it out there. I want to have my own business so I have more time to be with my family, I want to travel and write books while I do what I love with my family. My «why» for getting up every morning is to never give up and show others that it is possible to really make it if you only are consistent with putting your message out there.

Your why is what fuels your body. Remind yourself every day why you do what you do. When you have something to celebrate, do it. When things feels bad then know your why for being in business. There will come a time when you feel so broken and left behind that you just want to scream at the world. Why haven't your dreams come true yet? It seems like everyone else in the online world have their success.

But you have to focus on yourself and your message. Even if they all have it and it seems like they have it all figure out, you don't have to feel miserable about it. Your time will come and it is just for you to make it happen. Know your why and stick to it when things feels heavy on your chest. People will be drawn to you when you really are clear on your message and you know deep down inside of you why you do what you do.

At times it can feel difficult to keep it up when no one buys from you or likes your facebook post. But you must not give up. Instead of giving up, you will give in and give it even more from yourself. Market more, blog more, push it out more. The only obstacle you have is that people don't know about you. You have to be that online star that feels comfortable shining in the spotlight. Why have you been hiding so far? The time is now for you to shine and take the stage. Your time has come and people will notice you. Are you afraid of letting yourself out there?

Many women are and that's why it is so important to take the spotlight away from you. Give it to the people you will serve and then they will turn it back at you and tell all their friends about how nice and fabulous you are in your job. They will turn to you and let all their friends and colleagues know about what kind of women you are.

Your «why» will be the only thing that will keep you going when things feels rough and hard. I know for sure that I have to remind myself at times that I'm in it for the long haul. It is easier to just have a regular 9-5 job with a steady income and just relax on the sofa at night. But what about your dreams then? What about all the people that don't get the help they need because you decided to give up?

Are you in it just for yourself or for them? To make money you have to connect with people. You have to give them hope and let them see that they can also make it if they really want it.

If you give up now then think about your future. Is this all there is to life? Are you not on this path because you are meant for so much more? You are. You are amazing and your «why» will keep you going. Write it down every single day and read it out loud. Talk about it. Remind yourself that you are here to help other people. You can take the uncertainty that comes with being in business for yourself, but you know that it is worth it in the end.

But when will the end come? It will come when you release yourself and unleash what is holding you back. For me now it is that I don't belive enough in myself to go BIG. I mean really big. I want to work with celebrities, have my own column in a magazine and be a best selling author on Amazon. There I said it.

How about you? What is holding you back right now? Why can't you have what they got? Why are you not the hot online star out there collecting customers like hot cakes?

Deep down inside of you is the answer to anything. You have to up level yourself and your mind to really believe enough in yourself to get there. You must also ask and take action. I take action every single day. Today I had a Skype call with a client, but after that I did not feel like doing anything. My writing is usually in the morning but I did not have time for that. So now I write. Do I feel like doing it? No. I feel like watching YouTube videos on other peoples amazing life and just relax and have fun.

But then I said to myself. What is the outcome of that? Nothing. What do you want? Get my 4th book written and become a bestselling author. Do I get that if I watch YouTube videos? No.

So I got to work and now I write with flow. I love writing and I always know my «why». I write to inspire others, it is also therapy for myself and I write because my big goal is to have over 100 published books on Amazon.

Think about this. If people buy 1 of my books and like it, don't you think they will buy more? Of course they will. And then I make money and I reach out to more people. I am happy about my life most of the time, but the daily struggle to find motivation and keep going is hard. Even if I love what I do it's hard. That's why you have to know why you do what you do.

The bigger picture will always get you unfocused when you do your small daily task. What point is there to get up in the morning to write if no one reads it? In the end your daily blogs, tasks, message will get noticed. If you really stick to it you will have a business, an online reputation that is amazing and clients will come to you.

But it's also an inside job you have to battle every single day. Many days I don't feel like doing my work. I feel uninspired, tired, flat, bored at life etc. But that is life. As an online entrepreneur you have to pick yourself up day after day and keep going. When it feels tough, when no one buys from you, when you are sick, when you are tired, when you are unhappy. Yes, you have to push your limits to the max. I have done it for months now. 4 books in 4 months, coaching clients, giving my all out there, blogs every day, 8 videos on YouTube every month, but it all is because I want to follow my passion and reach more people.

Why? Because I want purpose, passion and flow in my business. I could do this all day long and my best advice for you is to keep going. If you only have 1 hour in the day you will succeed no matter what. If money is tight then find a solution. I will never ever go back to a boring and uninspiring 9-5 job. I actually miss my colleagues but now I can show them that if they want to follow their passion they can do it. Just like I did.

You are here for a reason, don't miss out on the big things in life just because you don't feel like it. You want the freedom, money, fame and creativity that comes with working for yourself. Then don't be afraid to put all of your gifts out there and just do it.

Write, talk, blog, use videos and keep going until you make it. You know when you will have success don't you?

You will have success when you see it in your mind and says that this is a done deal. You claim it. Then you do your daily tasks like everyone else out there. But you do it for a bigger cause, you are out there helping other change their lives. You will have success when you give in and says that this is me. Like me or hate me. I am coming your way and you better watch out.

Business is not that hard when you decide on what you want, that you deserve to have it and then go out there and attract the right people in.

I love my clients. Talking to them on Skype gives me so much joy. I thank them for being so honest with me and letting me know all their obstacles and why they don't believe enough in themselves. I attract the right ones because I am so honest in what kind of people I like to work with. They are amazing women just like me. Mothers, spiritual women, 90s fans, crazy corporate bitches and animal lovers. And then there is you. You have bought my book. I love you honey. You are in it to win it. Just because of you and that you read this book I can make a living helping other women find their true path to happiness and live a life on their own terms.

I will also be a speaker for the animals. No more cruelty in this world. There are no reasons that they should suffer for our cause. My next book will be about that and I know it's gonna be a bestseller just because I have claimed it.

Claim what you want and make it a done deal. Know you why and speak your truth about what you like and love. Be bold. Honest. Be you. Love yourself because you are good enough just the way you are.

Why? Because you want it. So then go out and take it. How? Claim it. Take action. Talk to people. Ask them for money for your services. Then repeat and repeat. Be you. Be yourself.

Know your «why» and stick to it when things feel rough. You can make it. I know you can. I'm waiting for you. Shine like a star in the online community now. I want to see you and applaud you for being yourself and making money being you.

How many of you are there out there? Non. So what are you waiting for? Yes, I know it can be hard to get over your fears and just do it. But listen honey. You only got one life. It's a good idea to start making the most of it now. Don't you agree?

CHAPTER 9: FIND OTHER STARS AND COLLABORATE

When you are out there in the online community and try to make a name for yourself, try to connect with other online stars you love. It can be celebrities, other online gurus, artists you like or other people you look up to. If they have a big audience they could promote you if you are a nice person and do your things right.

I don't mean that you should suck it up and try to be liked by everyone, but it is easier if you try to connect and collaborate with people that are bigger stars than you right now. If you believe in the same cause like animal rights, vegan food, fashion or other things then tell them why you like them and do whatever you can to get noticed.

Don't feel that this is dishonest because it's not. If you really like them, you say it and stalk them in a nice way. Think about now what kind of celebrities you like and who you would like to have a collaboration together with. I know this is a scary step to take and I myself is now up leveling my business. I am so sick and want to throw up when I now know that I have to connect with celebrities. Then it comes up «who am I?» «Am I that good?». I don't believe enough in myself when things getting a little bit more uncomfortable. I hate it actually but the thing you fear the most in your business, is actually then thing you should do.

Sounds horrible to go after something you fear, but that is the only way you can grow your business. If you want a quick and fast road to success, then learn from the big ones and connect with them. People are mostly nice to other people so there are no reason you should not ask for what you want.

You are just as good as all the others out there. Why you have not been discovered yet as the online star you are is only because there are something that is holding you back. Ask yourself what it is. Is it fear? That you don't believe enough in yourself? That you feel you don't have what it takes? Do you feel that when you get discovered it will be so much more work and you would not see your family? Or is it just because you actually don't want it that much?

It's important that you find out what is stopping you and try to work on your beliefs about yourself. Then you connect with your online stars you want to work with or learn from. You can follow them on Facebook, Twitter, Instagram, Periscope or wherever they are hanging out. Write to them, comment on their posts, connect, ask questions and show yourself and that your are really interested in their work.

Of course they will notice you and connect back. That is what will happen no doubt about it. I have had big makeup companies contacting me because I have retweeted their stuff and supported them in anyway I can. You can do the same for your online stars and be kind and generous with everything you say and do. You do this only with them you really look up to and want to work with.

Today make a list of 2-3 companies, online stars and people you love that you can follow. Like their Facebook page, Twitter, Instagram, Periscope, Youtube channel and connect with them in an honest way. The more time you have to connect to them, faster you will get results. And if you want to have a collaboration or work with them, guess what? You have to ask. If you don't ask the answer will always be no!

So get of your high horse and do something about it now. Today. I have reached out to 3 companies that I want to work with. One said no and the other 2 I have not heard back from. Do I give up. Not at all. I will send another email or make them a call. Everything is figuroutable as Marie Forleo says. You can figure it out and yes you can make it as an online star. Make connections and do it today. There will never come a time when you are ready for it. You will never be ready. Trust me. I'm not ready for big things coming up, but I say to myself get a grip and get over yourself. Just do it.

What is the worse thing that can happen? That they say no or that you never get a response? Then pick yourself up and make another call, send another email. People that never give up will have success no matter what. And you are now on your way so this is your next step. You have to up level if you want success. I know that I am afraid now how far I can take my business. I want a VA, an assistant for styling and I want to work more in London. I love styling clients, but I will only work with vegan clothing. It's not many stylist out there that does this and that frightens me. I'm the only one out there so that's why I feel a little bit fear to really go out and do it.

But sometimes you just have to pick yourself up and be your best friend. Tell yourself that you can make it and that you are ready for it. Right now is the time for you to go after your dreams. You can be the one that stand up for something big that no one else does. It can be hard, but if you follow your heart and do what feels close to your passion in life, then you are up for something big.

Ask yourself if you are ready. Because I know that I'm not ready. I'm holding myself back right now because I feel a fear about my up level. I know that I have to face my biggest obstacles in life and I have to work a lot to make it. But as I say you can figure everything out and become known for the thing you want. You can be a coach, an author, a stylist, a web designer. Whatever you can dream about you can have.

For so many years I have been longing to work for myself and not go to a 9-5 job. But now when I actually do that I don't really see how lucky I am. I miss my colleagues but everything else is ok to have left. I should be jumping around every single day that I can do what I love and make a living from it. Instead I am afraid to go after my really big dreams because what if? Yes, what if is the question that comes up with us women.

What if it doesn't work out? But what if it works out? What can happen for you then? Everything that happens in life, I believe, happens for a reason. I am free now and so are you. If you still work in a 9-5 job, that is ok. Be happy that it pays the bills. Sometimes I miss the 9-5 job because the money came so easily in. I knew what to do but it was not so inspiring.

To go after your dreams are inspiring, but also really hard. I feel it many times that I just want to give up. I have had some success up until now but I am ready for so much more. I say. But do I do something about it? I am scared. Scared that when it happen I will never be the same person. But that is my choice isn't it? Of course I can be the same person that likes shopping, reading inspiring books, connect with interesting people and feel free and alive.

I know that big things are happening for me and for you. If you have bought this book then I know that something draw you to it. I don't think that is a coincident and I know that you are that kind of person that believes you can have it all and go after it.

You are like me. A crazy bitch that thinks you can have it all on your terms. Every single day. But you can honey. You can make money being you. You can be a hot online star. You can look amazing. You can feel free and alive. You can be romantic and love your husband. You can handle kids and a business. You can be yourself in any way you like.

You have it in you to make it. You are the next online star. Connect with the people you like and see what happens. If you believe in the same cause and do something big in this world, then you can both make really big things happening.

No one can do it all alone. Go get them tiger. Now!

CHAPTER 10: MAKE MONEY JUST BY BEING YOU

You have tried the long and boring path now to make money. You have been following the proven steps to success but nothing has worked for you. How do I know? Honey I've been there. I have been trying to be like everyone else out in the online market place. Following the proven steps but nothing has worked out. It wasn't before I really got clear on what I want and how I want it that things started to roll.

Now I have big things coming up for me. So big that I want to puke, but that is just an upper limit problem you know? You can definitive make money just by being you. I love being myself and finding the right client to work with. They started signing up for my Discovery Calls when they saw that I was a real person. I was not bragging about how much money I make. I don't do that. But I can do it now to let you be clear. I have no debt beside of my mortgage. And my mortgage is not that big. I have 2 cars, own a holiday house in beautiful Lofoten where I can relax and write on my books. I have a closet full of designer clothing I love. Not that much, because I like to combine cheap clothing with more quality stuff.

I feel rich because I have two lovely girls. A husband that supports me following my passion and I have a mother that loves me. I have always been good with money and all the courses and coaches I have been investing in I have paid for with my own money. No credit card. I only own 1 credit card! That's it. But I have always felt that way that I want to have money in my bank account and that money was not something that I should brag about in my marketing. The real people that I work with can get to know me in that way if they want to.

When you put yourself out there with the good and the ugly, the right people will be drawn to you. They will see that you are authentic in everything you do. That you are a real human being with flaws like everyone else out there. We all feel fear. We all feel that we're not good enough. That is something that is built in our self belief. But you can do something about it. Don't listen in on your fears. Just do the stuff you love anyway and be yourself in all the things you do.

Make it hard for others to copy you when «being you» is what you sell. Do it in the things you create, the things you sell, the way you speak, the way you act and work with people. Then they can't complain, you will never have them to ask for their money back and you got to make money just by being you.

Life and business will be so much easier when you decide that you will make it just by being you. The crazy, the bad, the ugly, the beautiful. Give them all of you in everything you do. When I started writing from my heart I created book after book. This is my 4th one and my 5th one is on my mind already. I love writing and people buy it. I will never stop writing because I know the right people will show up. They will notice me. They do already.

Are you ready to step it up and be yourself? What is it that you hold yourself back with? Is there something that is on your mind that you would love to talk about and write about? Do it.

Don't think about the consequences. We are not on this earth to please everyone. We are here to show others that they must wake up and start being themselves in everything they do. Why else do we live? Just to make money and die? I don't think so.

You have everything you need to have success, fame and fortune. The more you give of your true self, the more you will sell, be popular and make more money. We both know that you are not here on earth just for the sake of making money. You are here to impact.

You want to be the next online star because you want to make an impact. You want to be seen and touch peoples heart. You can do that. The most authentic people touch you in your heart. They get to you because they are themselves. Think about the last time you cried over something. Was is not because someone said something that touched your heart? It could have been in a good way or a bad way. Either way it touched your heart.

When you first start to be yourself you have to be consistent with it. Don't give your all in just one blog post then think that people will flock to you. As in everything else you have to show up every single day and do your work. That is the fastest way to success. Most women hold themselves back and don't want to be seen in a special way. But you cannot decide on how people look at you. You are not here to be liked by everyone. You are here to be liked by your tribe. Your fans. Your online followers.

Making money online is the easiest thing to do. Everyone could do it. But the only thing that stops people is that either they give up to soon, or they don't go all in. If you never give up and go all in with your business, you can't fail. How many years it will take? I don't know. Decide when you will have it done. If you say 3 month then yes, definitive. Do it. But when you have claimed it, don't go back and start looking for profs that it hasn't happen yet. Look for profs after 3 months. Don't look after just one week.

The only check in you should do every single day is this. «Am I authentic and myself»? «Do I overthink too much»?

All the other stuff is just fluff. The steps. The proven things to success will never be proven for you. If you not have had success before, then why do you think that following more steps will get you to your final destination. But what is your final destination?

You have to love what you do and love every part of it. The god, the bad and the ugly. Life is not a walk in the park and it's not that easy to keep going day after day.

But it is much more easier to just live life on your terms and show up as yourself every single day if you are just being you. Give them days when you feel down. Give them inspiration when you are on your highs. Give them the shit that no one talks about. Then they will connect, then you will be known and then you will definitive be seen in the online market place.

If you show up every day with your message in a blog post, facebook post, podcast, Periscope you will reach more people, you will make more connections, more sales. People will notice you as that chick who goes after what she wants and they will follow you. Look up. You are the next big online star out there. I feel that time has come for you to step it up a notch. You have to be comfortable hiding out in the online community. Don't.

Show up every day. Be yourself. Make money just by being you.

I know that you got what it takes, but you have to believe in yourself and put yourself out there. Do it more and in as many platforms as you can.

Let no one stop you from having it all.

You are the next online star!

ABOUT THE AUTHOR

Camilla Kristiansen is a Kick-Ass Mentor for women who dream about living their freedom laptop lifestyle.

Growing up in a small town called Reine in Lofoten Camilla started her journey with a degree in Bachelor of Commerce/Business Studies. Later on she followed her passion in fashion and started her own business in 2010 as a stylist. Camilla now lives in Bodø, Norway with her two children and a supportive husband. She is traveling the World with her VIP days to nice locations like London, Paris, Milan & Oslo. Camilla is ready to change women all around the world with her coaching online company. Her mission is to help other women live their dream life with a business and lifestyle beyond their wildest dreams. She's all about taking action everyday to make your dreams come true and use your imagination to make it happen FAST.

Connect with Camilla and download her free gifts at http://camillakristiansen.com/freegift

Come and be my friend on Facebook and follow my travels and laptop lifestyle at https://www.facebook.com/pages/Camilla-Kristiansen/855052677847198

Buy all my other books here: https://camillakristiansen.com/

books/

Make me happy!

I will be so happy and appreciative if you'd consider leaving me feedback on this book. It will help me share my message and make other women get to know this book that can change their life in a positive way. It will only take you 2 min to leave a feedback on Amazon.

Thank you so much!

Hugs and kisses from Camilla

www.ingramcontent.com/pod-product-compliance
Lightning Source LLC
Chambersburg PA
CBHW021510210526
45463CB00002B/966